NATIONAL
GEOGRAPHIC

D0503590

Nature's SOLUTIONS

PIONEER EDITION

By Leslie Hall and Phyllis Edwards

CONTENTS

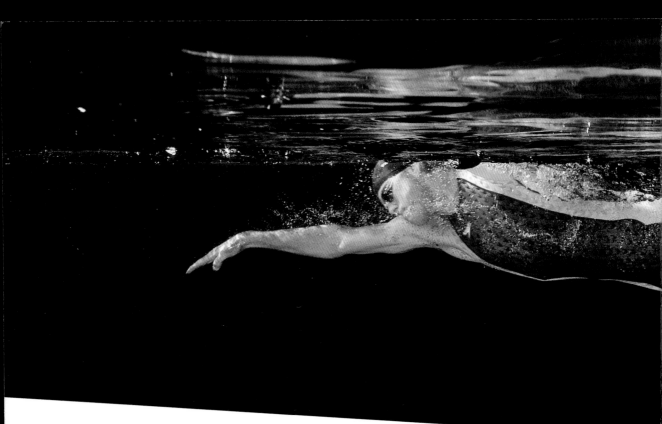

Nature's
SOLUTIONS

By Leslie Hall

People like to make things work better, faster, and cleaner. Luckily, they can turn to nature for some great ideas.

WE CAN LEARN A LOT FROM NATURE. Plants and animals are **efficient**. They don't waste energy. They are designed to live in balance with Earth. So people study nature to solve common problems.

PROBLEM: How can we help people swim faster?

SOLUTION: Study a shark's skin.

Even the sports world studies nature. For example, engineers used **biomimicry** to help swimmers.

A shark's skin has scales shaped like teeth. These "teeth" have tiny grooves between them. Water flows smoothly through the grooves. Engineers made a swimsuit based on sharkskin. It helped people swim faster than ever.

Bird Beaks and Bullet Trains

PROBLEM: How can we build quieter and better trains?

SOLUTION: Copy the shape of the Kingfisher bird's beak.

Kingfisher birds eat fish. They dive headfirst into lakes and rivers to catch their prey. Their long beaks help them dive into the water with almost no splash. This gave a Japanese engineer an idea. He helped make one of the fastest trains in the world.

The bullet train is fast. But when the train came out of tunnels, it made a lot of noise. The engineer thought about the bird. He changed the front end of the train. He gave it a pointed shape like the bird's beak. Now the train is quieter. It uses less power, too!

Gecko Grip

PROBLEM: How can we build robots that can climb walls?

SOLUTION: Study the tiny toes on a lizard's foot.

Geckos can cling to walls and ceilings. What's their sticky secret? It's the tiny hairs on their feet and toes. Each hair splits 100 to 1,000 times.

This means the lizard holds on at a billion different points! Also, the ends of the hairs are shaped like spoons. They give geckos a super strong grip.

Engineers studied geckos' hairy toes. Then they made a robot called Stickybot. The robot can climb up walls. Someday, the robot may even help rescue people.

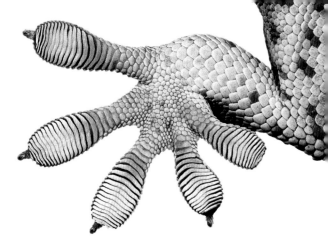

Fancy Feet. *Scientists studied geckos' toes. Then they made a robot that can climb up walls.*

Sleek Shape. *The shape of a kingfisher's beak inspired the front end of this bullet train.*

5

Lessons From Leaves

PROBLEM: How can we keep the outside of buildings clean?

SOLUTION: Study how rainwater rolls off a leaf.

A lotus leaf is covered with tiny bumps. Those bumps keep the leaf clean and dry. How? They keep rainwater from touching the leaf.

They also make the drops bead up into a ball. The balls of water roll right off the leaf. Dust and dirt roll off the leaf with them.

Engineers **researched** the lotus leaf to create special paint. The paint can clean itself! Dirt rolls off the paint just like it rolls off the leaf. Thanks to the lotus, we may soon be able to keep ice off airplane wings. We may even learn new ways to keep clothes dry!

Keeping Clean. *Engineers studied lotus leaves. They used what they learned to make a new type of paint.*

Ideas Take Flight. *Engineers study bombardier beetles to build better jets.*

Beetle Juice

PROBLEM: How can we re-start a jet engine while the plane is flying?

SOLUTION: Just do what some beetles do.

When the bombardier beetle is scared, gases fill part of its abdomen. The gases make heat and pressure. The pressure quickly grows. Then boiling liquid and steam shoot out of the beetle's body.

What does this have to do with jet engines? High in the air, the engines may shut down. So pilots need engines that turn back on in mid-air.

Engineers are studying the beetle. They want to learn how it makes and shoots the spray so fast. They want to make new engines, based on the bombardier beetle.

Fuel-Saving Fish

PROBLEM: How can we build cars that use less gasoline?

SOLUTION: Look closely at the shape of a fish.

The shape of a boxfish lets it move through water quickly. Engineers copied the fish's smooth shape to design a new car. The new car is shaped like the fish. Because of the shape, the car is more efficient. It uses less fuel.

Would you like to find better solutions for everyday problems? Look around. Ask questions. Which creatures inspire you?

WORDWISE

biomimicry: imitating nature to solve problems

efficient: does not waste energy

research: to get information about something

Flying Snakes

Help Build Better Aircraft

BY
PHYLLIS EDWARDS

How do you design a better gliding machine? You study flying snakes, of course! That's what Jake Socha does. He studies the ways animals move. For years, he has studied the paradise tree snake. This is a snake that "flies." He wants to understand the way this animal moves.

Meet the Paradise Tree Snake

Many animals fly. But the paradise tree snake is the best animal flier. When it leaps from a tree, it can land many yards away! It sails through the air better than flying squirrels, flying lizards, or flying fish. Only birds fly better than paradise tree snakes.

The word "fly" is not quite correct. It's true that these snakes can move themselves through the air. But snakes do not have wings. They cannot move up through the air to a higher place. So it's better to say that the paradise tree snake glides.

But how does the snake do this? That's what Jake Socha studies.

All the Right Moves

Jake Socha records paradise tree snake flights on film. He uses these images to answer his questions.

Socha found that the snake does not just drop down from a branch. It actually leaps out from the branch horizontally. This way it starts from the highest possible point. Next it dives down for a few seconds. This helps it gain speed. Then it levels out and glides to a landing.

Socha also discovered that the snake controls its flight by moving its body from side to side. This helps it stay in the air longer and to steer itself to where it wants to land.

A Snake in Flight

Leaping from branch ➡ Diving to gain speed ➡ Moving to stay aloft and control direction

Flying Facts

Scientific Name:
  Chrysopelea paradisi
Class: reptile
Size: Up to 4 feet long

Range: Southeast Asia
Habitat: trees in Southeast Asia
Diet: meat-eating: rodents, small lizards

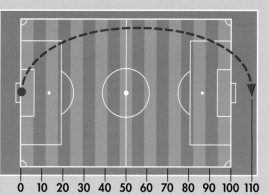

Gliding Distances: up to 330 feet, or 110 yards
Flying Snake's Path: 110 yards
Soccer Field: 100 yards

0 10 20 30 40 50 60 70 80 90 100 110   YARDS

Challenges and Responses

Most wild animals share a big problem: predators! For paradise tree snakes, flying is an excellent solution. When a large bird comes too close, the snake can move away quickly. When a giant lizard climbs the snake's tree, it can glide to another tree.

Animals have another big problem. They must find food every day. This takes a lot of time and energy! The paradise tree snake solves this problem by flying. When it is hungry, it can fly to many trees to find food.

The Future of Flight

How will people use what we have learned about flying snakes? Will they build new kinds of airplanes? Someday will people travel in spaceships modeled on flying snakes? Only time will tell.

Flying squirrel

Key Questions

Jake Socha has found the answers to these key questions.

1 *How does the snake's body change as it flies?*

An animal like the flying squirrel uses its legs and extra skin to create "wings."

But a snake doesn't have legs. Instead, the snake bends its skeleton. This changes the shape of its whole body from the inside out!

2 *How does its shape help the snake stay in the air?*

Scientists looked at photographs of a snake in flight. They compared it to images that show air flowing around the snake's body as it flies. They found that the snake's body looks a lot like an airplane wing.

Both the wing of an airplane and the flying snake's body have a similar shape. This shape is called an airfoil. This shape keeps flying objects in the air. The snake's entire body is like a long, narrow wing!

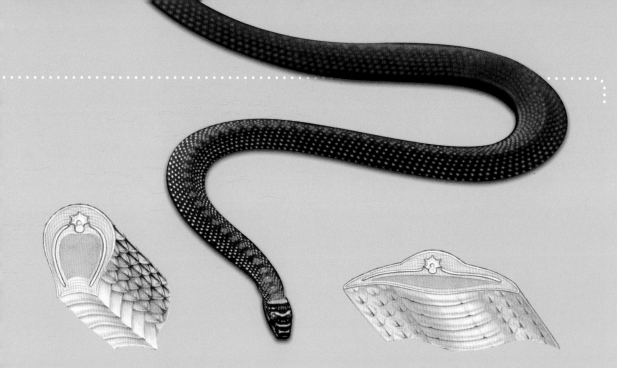

Not Flying. *Most of the time, the flying tree snake's body is round like a garden hose.*

Flying. *When it flies, the snake bends its ribs out from the center of its body. This gives the body a concave shape. From below, it looks like the snake has sucked in its stomach!*

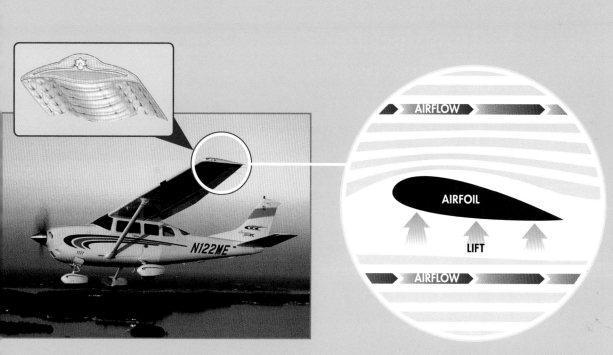

AIRFLOW

AIRFOIL

LIFT

AIRFLOW

N122ME

Special Shape. *When a snake flies, its body is a lot like the shape of an airplane wing. This special shape helps the snake stay up in the air.*

Wild Ideas

Let your ideas run wild. Then answer these questions.

1 How are plants and animals naturally efficient?

2 How do people use plants and animals to solve everyday problems?

3 Name three inventions that use biomimicry.

4 How does the paradise tree snake fly even though it doesn't have wings?

5 How does Jake Socha learn about paradise tree snakes?